Requiem for the Intercity 125

Poems of travel and change

by

TJW Thornes

Poems of Travel & Change

WASH HOUSE PUBLISHING

Poetry

Published by Wash House Publishing 2018

Printed on demand by CPI Group.
The CPI Group is committed to the prevention of pollution and continual improvement to reduce our effect on the environment.

Copyright © Tobias Thornes, 2018.
All Rights Reserved. All or part of this publication may be reproduced, reprinted or otherwise disseminated only when accompanied by acknowledgement of the author.

Produced with the aid of, and available from www.completelynovel.com

Requiem for the Intercity 125

Contents

Foreword	4
Tracks of Time	8
The Campaign for the Comfortable Train	10
Leaving	13
Returning	15
Hereford Bound	17
On the Road	19
A May Lane	20
The Severn Valley Way	22
Departure	24
Falling	25
Into Silence	27
Embers	30
The Last Survivor	32
Requiem for the Intercity 125	34
On the Great Western Railway	38
Goodbye	40
Postscript for the 125	42

Poems of Travel & Change

Foreword

Travel is an inescapable part of existence. Most of us travel spatially between several places every day, near or far, and we all have journeys that we enjoy and journeys that we dread. But no one can avoid the travel through time that we all undergoing, all the time, no matter how much we might want to. Sometimes, the journey through our lives seems exciting, the future brims with opportunity and we look forward to the coming of the new day, to a new start, to a fresh understanding or a new relationship. At other times, we long to stay still, to cherish a moment of joy that it seems will so easily shatter, or to retain our diminishing youthfulness in the face of inevitable ageing and decay. And at the worst of times, the destination ahead looks bleak and drear, and we may wish to give up on the journey altogether.

This collection of poems is inspired by the emotions aroused by travel through both space and time, both real and imaginary. The title piece, *Requiem for the Intercity 125*, sets the tone for the whole volume, in that it describes a journey in space but also a passage through time, mixing together a yearning to retain present joys with apprehension about the future and a feeling of regret for something that is about to be lost. The poem was written in October 2017, at a time when the Intercity 125, an iconic train that had provided the author with countless hours of joy rushing up and down the Cotswolds railway line, was slated for imminent replacement. The publication of this volume in December 2018 corresponds with what is expected to be the final month of that train's usage on the line. It will be sorely missed, and not only by me, and the poem is intended as a memorial and a tribute to what has become more of a 'friend' than a type of vehicle.

Some of the poems in this volume are intentionally light-hearted, especially the somewhat farcical *Campaign for the Comfortable Train*, amidst its joking approach are many serious points that I wanted to be heard. The same can be said for *On the Great Western Railway*, composed amidst the same mixture of sadness and anger that fuelled the *Requiem*, and partially intended as a riposte to the railway for making the, I would argue, entirely unnecessary and regrettable decision to sweep away the old and usher in the new. It is certainly the case that travel by rail has lost much of its romance, comfort and attractiveness as charm has given way to economic efficiency in recent years. Perhaps these poems will make some of us rethink what we are doing to our railways; perhaps not.

Rail travel has long been a favourite pastime of mine, and *Tracks of Time* and *Hereford Bound* express something of the thrill that it has given me in recent years and the nostalgia that it can excite. As well as the trains themselves changing in ways I regret, train journeys have marked out some of the major changes in my life, as alluded to in *Leaving* and, on a somewhat more optimistic note, *Returning*, which utilise the train journey as a metaphor for life's motion through changing scenes.

When travelling any significant distance in England, one is bound to encounter many different landscapes that evoke different eras of time. For one hailing, as I do, from the countryside, the most obvious observation is the transition from a realm largely dominated by nature – woods, streams, fields that man has planted but nature has grown – to a more modern, artificial environment sculpted by humans. With urbanisation has come a radical change in lifestyles that has both positive and negative repercussions for the quality of life enjoyed by both humans and other animals. *A May Lane*, *Into Silence* and *Falling* all take up the theme of lament for ways of life, ways of being and interacting with nature, and indeed species of animal that have all become extinct in a somewhat alien modern world. They remain only as distant memories, faded imprints in the landscape that we may never be able to revive, having travelled far beyond our roots on the tracks of modernisation.

Part of our spirit as humans, I believe, still dwells in and longs for the ages-old traditions that have been swept aside, like a certain out-dated type of train, on this societal journey. Perhaps more obvious casualties of the modern world, and specifically modern-day travel, are the many victims of so-called 'road kill' that lose their lives every day. Sadness for one such animal, battered beyond all recognition, was what inspired *On the Road*.

Finally, but perhaps closest to my heart, are three poems tinged by the sense of loss that we all experience as a result of death, old age and decay. *The Severn Valley Railway* is dedicated to a very dear friend with whom, before his very untimely death at the age of twenty-one, I often enjoyed sharing travels across Britain and across multiple stages of life that I now must undertake alone. The loneliness of life ebbing away, as youthfulness fades out on the journey that none of us can pause or put off, runs through *Embers*, and the undeniable notion that we must leave much of what we love behind is the theme of my final piece, *Goodbye*.

It is my dearest wish that you will enjoy reading these poems – whether they invoke feelings happy or sad – and sharing with me some of my meagre reflections on life, time, travel, change, and loss.

    T J W Thornes
    4th December 2018

Poems of Travel & Change

Tracks of Time

Chugging along my favourite line
On a winter's afternoon,
Under a silky, cloud-cast sky
The light is strangely yellow,
Like a thin veneer of copper
Cast across the countryside.
And all is peaceful, empty,
Waiting for the spring.

Here are cosy cottages,
Muggy fields and thickets
Of Worcestershire, Gloucestershire,
Oxford ambling by.
There's the path we followed
One fine day in one lost summer,
Between the Marsh and Kingham,
Where a long-lost station stood.

Windows down,
On the slow train worries float away.
We might have gained a hundred years
Or more of time;
Almost I can hear
The steaming steamer's stutter,
Smell the burning coal-dust –
When the railway line was new,

Requiem for the Intercity 125

And a magic dragon
Moved beneath this same spacious sky,
When a fresh industrial roar
Disturbed the bird-sung branches,
When Adlestrop was more
Than just the memory of a poem.

Poems of Travel & Change

The Campaign for the Comfortable Train

Why should it be such a pain,
Nowadays, to catch a train?

I'm fed up with sitting in a fridge,
On a seat more like a ridge,
Designed, it seems, to make you stand –
Or kneel and pray.
If I wanted a pew I'd go in a church –
And I wouldn't have to sit there all day.

I'm fed up with lifeless electric voices
On about baggage and 'gaps'
And stations they can't pronounce –
Why can't they just have a person to announce
The stops?

I'm fed up with feeling travel-sick
'Cos they say fresh air's no longer slick.
This isn't the Bay of Biscay in the rain –
It's a train!
And trains without toilets –
Whose idea was that?

Requiem for the Intercity 125

What are you supposed to do,
On a train where there's no loo,
And no opening windows too,
When you come to want to spew
Back up your cup of tasteless tea
That cost you two pounds seventy –
And not just from disgust
To be trapped in such a cage!
Oh, how it makes me rage!

So I'm starting a campaign –
The campaign for the comfortable train.

It must have seats soft enough to sit in it
For more than a minute.
It must not have a computerised voice,
And for goodness sake must offer the choice
Of windows open or closed:
To frigid, recycled air that smells of sick
I'm totally opposed.

Diesel, electric, steam –I don't care
As long as it gets me there
Without wishing I'd never set off
Or needing to sleep it all off.
If it's a bit late, I won't complain –
If it's a comfortable train.

It won't be packed like a cattle truck:
I don't mind standing, but rather not stuck
In the midst of a fretting, sweating throng
Unable to get off before more pile on.

You can take your vomity Voyager and drive it off a cliff!
You class 800s? Throw 'em in the Thames –
Or better still, despatch them down
To Dawlish in a storm.
I'd rather sit on the roof
If it wasn't so uncouth.

The intercity 125 –
Now there's a train I could survive,
Before they sealed the windows up
And packed them off to Inverness.
Oh, why is it more and more of a pain
To catch a comfortable train?

Requiem for the Intercity 125

Leaving

At first, the leaving was slow.
Sunshine on an empty country platform,
Rails almost humming with the heat.

A bird sang. The signal clattered,
Sounds well-known, my own, heard where my feet
Have stood a thousand times before.
This quiet corner, Home.

Down the line, a familiar face appears
And tugs me back to crisp-cool mornings and
Sweaty afternoons, across the years,
When never long or far I roamed.

The carriage stops, starts. For a time
We roll on down that well-known line.
The sleepy town recedes into fields of dreams;
Soon these fields will fill my dreams I know.

This luscious summer sun-kissed plain,
My heart, to memory's shadow now retires.
Each tree, each thicket I have loved:
I watch them pass. Leaving.

We stop anon at stations I have known
So long. But then go on.
The country train that rocked me
From my cradle thrusts me now into

Poems of Travel & Change

The busy city, where rushing feet pace all directions
And the air clams in the closed-in heat.
And the quiet plain, left far behind,
Knows nothing of me now.

Leaving. To a faster train I change,
To race me through the sunny afternoon.
Fields, houses rush away, and deeper
Into foreign lands I stray

Where sunshine scorches buckling rails
And bakes the waiting platforms, and above
Unseen, a harsh bird wails.
And all I know has vanished

Like the breeze, far away.

Returning

June. Spread out in all its brave, young green
Unbruised, as yet, by hotter suns
The summer promised with its long, light days.
The sense of a beginning hung around –
A gust of gladness through the sleepy air
As the journey, long withheld, began,
And we, at last, to freedom ran
Upon the rumbling rails.

Eight slipped into nine.
And still the sun long shadows cast
On golden fields made fiery, while hills
A hazed horizon formed and clouds played
In the sky, casting light and shade
Upon the glowing ground beneath.
In that bright light, the shaggy reefs
That make the forests of

The North rested, in the beauty of
A thousand verdant shades, and so
We rattled on, past forms and meadows
Which, bleak and bare, had shivered through long
Winter nights, now utterly reborn
In early summer's sweet delights
Of days. This world bore different sights
To those to which the drizzled journey up bore witness.

Poems of Travel & Change

The sky relaxed to deeper blue
As we hurried further south,
Past empty platforms, luminous, in the last
Luscious light, and all at once
The future stretches as a long summer dream,
In this twilight: the beginning
Of a new, still brighter day.

Requiem for the Intercity 125

Hereford Bound

Coming up the Malvern line on a sunlit summer's morning,
Creation's cradle lies about in beauty unsurpassed.
In dappled cool lies Droitwich Spa soon after the dawning,
Where down the winding tree-hung lanes through pretty fields I passed

To catch the train, and with the clatter of a signal
The shunting beast propelled us on our way
Past houses hushed, and through the open country,
'Neath Worcester's spires to see the starting day.

There the bridge, by skilful art, Majestic
Spans the river, road and banks alike,
To bear us to the land where hills replace hedges
And from far and wide they come to ride and hike

And see the splendour of two unrivalled counties
Laid out as a feast before their open eyes.
But not for us: deep beneath the Malvern hills we dived
And shot out into fresh delight beyond
To wind our way through fields and farms and tiny sleeping stations
To reach at last the place of which we'd grow so fond.

Then unknown, fresh and new it gleamed before us:
Hereford, the city hidden on the fringe of Wales.
And there, the great father-like cathedral
Beside whose tranquil pool of peace all other building
pales!

Here alone, the perfect culmination
Of this, our travel through nature's finest trove!
Man's best monument of God and truth this nation
Has with hands of love and care composed.
Man and nature, with love by love empowered
In these two counties perfectly reposed.

On the Road

I couldn't tell what it was.
Lying in the road, flattened and re-flattened
By a thousand passes of rolling-pin tyres.

Once it had life in it, no doubt, once breath
Must have filled the lungs that somewhere
Form part of the pulp that remains – before the death
That must have struck so suddenly.

A quiet hour of the night,
A poorly chosen time for flight
Across the road, and then –
Indeed, so suddenly it strikes these days,
The end.

So carelessly the body is abandoned, not picked bare
By nature's scavengers here, for few dare
To risk the road.

Yes, this was a creature once, but nothing now remains
Except a flattened residue and fading, sickly stains.

Poems of Travel & Change

A May Lane

Muddling through England in the middle of May,
Down dusty lane sprinkled with snow,
Where bright blossoms gleam in the long light of day
And sweet scents on blest breezes blow.

I from my hedgerows and sleepy woods stir,
Roused by the tune of the town,
But tonight I'll be back from the weary world's whir
When the sun makes his merry way down.

Though the road may ramble, rocky and long,
I'll ponder, wherever I roam,
The sweet honeysuckle, the blackbird's late song,
Waiting to welcome me home.

The short Sunday train shunts slowly and late,
Of rushed weekday worries relieved:
The hourly shuttle has time now to wait,
By the late-comer gladly received.

Mild is the May air, all windows down!
The pretty spring smiles as we pass,
Brimming with green where of late there was brown,
With daisies and buttered-gold grass.

So Wonderful Worcestershire shows off its gems,
This mellowest month, sunlit spring,
The golden oaks glowing with forget-me-not hems,
Where faint bluebells still shadows fling.

Requiem for the Intercity 125

This is my world, as with wonder I gaze,
Past glad yellow pastures we wind;
No city of splendour can ever amaze
Like the life of the land left behind!

Into the torrid town, tardy we crawl
Where trees become turrets and towers,
But the richer the banquet of pride, come the fall,
The more turgid the taste when it sours.

Thus into the bare, barren brick-lands I came;
I answered my summons from Rome,
But ever my heart lingered still on that lane,
Waiting to wind be back home.

The Severn Valley Way

Steaming down from Highley,
Wondering at the view,
Smothered by the steam smoke,
And thinking, friend, of you.

It doesn't seem a moment
Since that hot August day,
When you and I last took our trip
On the Severn Valley Way.

Steaming on to Bridgnorth,
A smile on your face,
Lulled by the poetic charm
Of the slow train's steady pace.

Still I hear your laughter,
Rippling through the air –
But the seat beside me's empty, now
That you're no longer there.

Three short years ago,
With all your plans and hopes:
Such bright thoughts for the future,
Now gone up in smoke.

My dear, dear companion,
I had no vague idea
That the next time down this railway line
You'd be no longer here.

Requiem for the Intercity 125

So I've come again to smell the steam,
This sunlit August day,
Remembering another life,
A brighter summer's day.

How many souls have left us,
Since this old train was new!
But I feel the loss of none, my friend,
As I feel the loss of you.

Departure

Why is this journey clouded so, in melancholy blue?
With such joy I journeyed late, dreaming dreams of you
When on that sunny afternoon I trundled down this track –
Now I struggle up again with shadows at my back.

Shadows of unspoken words, and things I might have done;
Memories of a time too short, a meeting just begun.
I came to you with happy glee upwelling from my heart,
But somehow busy goings-on kept us still apart.

I wish I'd not upset you, didn't want to interfere.
I wish we could have parted with a smile and not a tear.
Now the pools of loneliness are dripping from my eyes,
A wish I could have stayed for fonder, honester goodbyes.

As the train takes me off into the dying afternoon,
I long to see you waving in the soft light of the Moon,
But now the night clings coldly with the dark fog of despair
As I look upon my folly, when I see there's no one there.

Here's my self-inflicted curse: to walk this world alone,
My heart so broke I fear I'll not again go joyful home.

Falling

A sense of falling.
Stones slip from the crumbling coast,
The vessel smashing on the floor
Will never prise another smile.

Spent, now, are the matches
That reignited memories,
Lost like papers carried
Through the window by the wind,

Or the jewel dropped in a moment on the beach
And for a lifetime missed.
Do broken bricks still bear the record
Of palaces pushed down?

Do the dingy dens, the drinking-holes,
The sticky clubs and shabby shops
They put up in their stead
Still harbour happy heirlooms

Of a place repaired?
Or, beneath the trim tarmac,
The benches tidy and bare,
The primly painted railings

That so neatly rail us in,
Has the magic disappeared?
Blown away,
And swept up with the leaves.

Poems of Travel & Change

Building Babylon from Jerusalem,
    The stolen stones
Won't bear the weight for long.

Requiem for the Intercity 125

Into Silence

The old field is quiet now,
Where once the haymen hummed,
A hundred voices ringing out
While the busy scythers strummed.

The old inn is quiet now,
Where many a weary day
Was ended in much merriment
Brought on by sweat and hay.

The old lane is quiet now,
Where once the wagons clopped,
And jaunts and taunts and playful words
By a hundred mouths were swapped.

The old stable's quiet now –
No horse's heavy breath,
No cursing of the ostler,
No cries of birth nor death.

The old mill is quiet now,
It's crushed its final grain.
Empty is the rotten store,
Open to the rain.

The old dairy's quiet now,
No more the maid's loud laugh,
Who knew each tit of every cow –
There's no more need for staff.

The old canal is quiet now,
Where bargemen's poles would clang,
The whispering wind the only voice
Where once they loudly sang.

The breakfast table's empty now,
No places left to set;
The thoughts and dreams of decades shared,
These tired walls forget.

The old woods are quiet now,
The children's voices stopped,
The playful birds are left alone
Now all the swings have dropped.

The old church is empty now,
The congregation grey,
And crumbling like the withered stone
Where none now come to pray.

The village green is quiet now,
For all the doors are shut,
The vales resound in verse no more
For all the chords are cut.

The aged hills are quiet now,
Stripped off, their songs of old,
Abandoned to the silence
Of the noise that now takes hold –

Requiem for the Intercity 125

Lifeless, and loveless,
The sighing rubber surf
And the mindless hum of dead machines
That labour on the turf.

The old graveyard's quiet now,
The choking grass grows long,
Where many merry mouths rot shut
And none take up the song.

Embers

Will you share with me, my love,
The burden of my years?
Will you firm my jellied heart
As dreams give way to fears?

In the dead dark of the morning,
When the warmth of love has gone –
Fading, like the stone-cold hearth
That yesternight blazed strong –

Will you hold my ageing hands
While the spark of youth dies out
And guide me through the slipping hours
Of days diseased with doubt?

Who overturned the hour glass?
Who wound on the clock?
Who took the box of life's delight
And smashed apart the lock,

And poured the contents, garbled,
And wasted on the floor?
Will you help me salvage from
The wreck of my lost store?

I, only I, it was,
Who burned my candle low.
My many days escaped like wax
Whose wane I could not slow.

Requiem for the Intercity 125

A hidden light, in empty rooms,
A fire that shone in vain.
When the flickering wick burns out,
Will you ease the pain?

We hurtle like a brakeless train,
E'er faster down the track;
Never can we linger,
Never may we slack,

Lonely as a falling star
That plumbs the depths of space,
Disgusted by the faults within
My own reflected face.

But another's light is beauty,
Another's presence, peace:
Oh, will you give me purpose,
Before my vain decease?

The Last Survivor

Sleep soft. Surrender to the night,
Your final night, your fears;
Your eyes will see no morning,
Will wake no more to tears.

You saw them choke and flounder,
You marked them, one by one;
Bitter is the sunshine now
That lights on you alone.

Sleep, sleep, your weary rest;
Your happy spring long past.
Lonely is the winter long
When you alone are last.

Happy were the endless days
When your kind was young;
Now your suffering sentience slips
Into oblivion.

Never more your voice will sing,
Silent stand the trees;
Your fancied form, your nounless name
But empty memories.

Sleep, sleep – your groves are gone,
Your summer stopped too fast;
Your palaces are vanished now,
And you alone are last.

Requiem for the Intercity 125

Close your eyes – your race is run,
And all your days are done.

Requiem for the Intercity 125

They've given him his notice.
They've settled on a time
To disappear, who forty years
Has trundled down this line.
The window-wipers dry his eyes,
The air-brakes sigh and hiss,
As round the bend once more they send
The friend that we will miss.

Say goodbye to fond farewells,
Waving from the door:
When he's gone the windows
Will not open any more.
Lean out and turn the handle;
Give a struggling friend a hand –
Soon electric doors
Will open for them on demand.

Hear him hum as up he starts,
Feel his gentle pulse;
Next time you'll be locked inside
A capsule sealed and false,
Where the wind's sweet whisper
Through the window will not blow;
The chance to feel the sun's soft rays
He offers you will go.

Requiem for the Intercity 125

Instead, an air-conditioned cage
Will race from A to B
And stop at all the stations
Where our friend we used to see.
Yes, he may be ageing now
But he isn't getting tired –
Oh, can't he have just one more chance
Before he's shot and fired?

"No!" says prancing progress,
And kicks him in the side.
"Let's trash this trundling tin-heap
And buy a better ride!
Who wants an ageing grandad?
He simply can't compete!
The new trains will be faster,
With bigger, softer seats.

"It isn't health and safety
To let in outside air,
And of your mushy memories,
I simply couldn't care.
People value comfort,
New toilets, tasty treats,
And the new trains will have all of this –
And bigger, softer seats."

But what of us who like to breathe,
The open window at the door?
"The new trains will not have
That backward feature any more.
See! The new electric screens,
Hear the automated voice!"
I'd rather suffer neither, thank you,
If I had the choice.

"Nonsense! People clamour for
The latest in our fleet.
And they must have a socket
At each bigger, softer seat."
And so he sauntered from me,
His fingers in his ears,
And I was left to board again,
Holding back the tears.

From Paddington to Hereford,
Into the setting sun,
The friendly train went rocking
On his final Cotswolds run,
From Oxford, Hanborough, Charlbury,
Kingham and the Marsh,
He hurtled straight past Honeybourne
To Evesham; Pershore passed,

Requiem for the Intercity 125

And whistled into Worcester,
Where I bade my friend goodbye,
Meandering to Malvern,
Thence to terminate – and die.
Oh, what happy memories forged
When you were still alive!
Oh please come back, bear your proud plaque,
'Beloved 1-2-5'!

Poems of Travel & Change

On the Great Western Railway

They don't do opening windows.
They don't do comfortable seats.
And can someone explain
Why this horrid new train
They've come up with so wholly retreats

From all that is good about travel,
From all that is comfort and style:
A shame it did seem
When they gave up on steam,
But this – why, this really is vile!

Till now I've been putting up with it,
Though many trains I've had to miss,
But now more and more
They've been changing, I'm sure –
This really is taking the Swiss!

I kept quiet when they changed the ten twenty,
The one twenty-three – not a jot.
But the day they mess
With the Cathedrals Express –
That's when the iron gets hot!

So graceful it slid down the platform,
The windows all down – such a charm,
With comfort inlaid,
And all British-made:
Change our old HST to your harm!

Requiem for the Intercity 125

We'll chase them out of the city,
We'll harry them out of the town!
They'll be racking their brains
Why they went into trains
By the time that our anger cools down!

We'll make them all sit for four hours
On cheap plastic seats by themselves,
While we pelt them with fruit
From the trolley on route
And sandwiches straight off the shelves!

We'll lock them where no windows open –
See how they like it all day,
Then we'll cancel their train,
Put it down to the rain,
And still the full fare make them pay!

We'll strap 'em on their new expresses,
Furnished with cheap plastic tat;
On time we shall send
Them off 'tip o' Land's End,
And there'll be an ending of that!

Yes, we'll pack 'em all off to the Ocean
With the whole horrid fleet of new trains,
Till they learn not to mess
With the Cathedrals Express
And perhaps on the way get some brains!

Goodbye

It isn't easy, this 'goodbye'
That I am ever saying,
And the pain of parting never
For this repetition seems to ease.
Goodbye old friend,
Goodbye to favourite places,
Lost, destroyed or far away,
Belonging to another life
To which I said farewell.

Goodbye to happy railway journeys,
Windows open wide,
Goodbye indeed to sweet goodbyes,
Waving as I gently drifted off
Along the rails.

Goodbye to where I lived and ate,
The daily rhythms of my life
That now lie dead like faded ruts
Or rusty, disused sidings
Overgrown with weeds.

Goodbye July, goodbye sweet June,
And goodbye all the former years
I knew and leave behind.
Those long-lost summers –
Wales and Cornwall,
Devon or deserted

Requiem for the Intercity 125

Wind-swept Northumbrian bays;
Castles on the headland
Crumbling slowly into dust
And long-abandoned monasteries
Empty and quiet.

Goodbye to all I've held so dear,
Goodbye to people gone like ghosts
Of lives I've lived before.
I don't recall the words with which
We parted last,
Who once had spoken every day.

The fruit trees fall I used to climb,
The shabby scenes of buildings, trains,
And meadows once were mine;
Goodbye to all – rebuilt, replaced,
Upgraded and for ever gone.

And yes, goodbye to youthful me,
For age will wear my limbs,
And stop my feet from dancing up
The hills I used to climb.
Goodbye, goodbye to everything –
Except the soul divine.

Postscript for the 125

Very soon they missed him,
When the air conditioning leaked,
And everyone complained about
The smaller, harder seats.
And when the new train sauntered up
Half an hour late,
Few among the passengers
Thought it worth the wait.

But Progress wouldn't hearken
To this first journey's curse:
They'd spent too many millions
Buying something worse
Than our beloved 1-2-5
They'd rushed to push aside
For fickle, flashy, tacky trains
While our old partner died.

Short was his resurgence;
As his whistle died away
We knew the train departing
Wouldn't come another day.

Requiem for the Intercity 125

So now we'll sit as captives,
Disgruntled and delayed.
A computerised apology
Through stale air is played,
But ever in our consciousness
The cancelled promise bleats:
'The new trains will be faster –
And with bigger, softer seats!'

Poems of Travel & Change

www.ingramcontent.com/pod-product-compliance
Lightning Source LLC
Chambersburg PA
CBHW062206100526
44589CB00014B/1982